ISBN 978-1-331-73432-1
PIBN 10227705

This book is a reproduction of an important historical work. Forgotten Books uses state-of-the-art technology to digitally reconstruct the work, preserving the original format whilst repairing imperfections present in the aged copy. In rare cases, an imperfection in the original, such as a blemish or missing page, may be replicated in our edition. We do, however, repair the vast majority of imperfections successfully; any imperfections that remain are intentionally left to preserve the state of such historical works.

English
Français
Deutsche
Italiano
Español
Português

www.forgottenbooks.com

Mythology Photography **Fiction**
Fishing Christianity **Art** Cooking
Essays Buddhism Freemasonry
Medicine **Biology** Music **Ancient
Egypt** Evolution Carpentry Physics
Dance Geology **Mathematics** Fitness
Shakespeare **Folklore** Yoga Marketing
Confidence Immortality Biographies
Poetry **Psychology** Witchcraft
Electronics Chemistry History **Law**
Accounting **Philosophy** Anthropology
Alchemy Drama Quantum Mechanics
Atheism Sexual Health **Ancient History**
Entrepreneurship Languages Sport
Paleontology Needlework Islam
Metaphysics Investment Archaeology
Parenting Statistics Criminology
Motivational

Power from on High.

DO WE NEED IT?
WHAT IS IT?
CAN WE GET IT?

enjamin

REV. B. FAY MILLS.

An address delivered at the Ninth International
Christian Endeavor Convention.

:: Fleming H. Revell ::

NEW YORK: | CHICAGO:
12 BIBLE HOUSE, ASTOR PLACE. | 148 AND 150 MADISON STREET.

= Publisher of Evangelical Literature =

1890

Entered according to Act of Congress in the year 1890 by

FLEMING H. REVELL

In the office of the Librarian of Congress, Washington, D. C.

POWER FROM ON HIGH.

DO WE NEED IT? WHAT IS IT?
CAN WE GET IT?

Our topic as it will be divided, will have reference, *first*, to the necessity for the Power from on high; *second*, to its character; and *third*, to the conditions of its attainment. In other words, Why do we need it? What is it? and, How may we get it?

There are three classes of people, and only three, who are Christians, in the church of Christ. The first class are in the church because they want to be saved; and what they mean by being saved is to get some sort of an entrance into what they call heaven. They are not at all concerned about the salvation of other people. There is another class of people who are concerned about their fellow men, but they believe that the way to bring them to God is by using such means as may lie in themselves, with wisdom and discretion, for this purpose. These people have a good deal to say about the latent power that exists in the church of God. There is no such thing. There is no power, latent or expressed, in the church of God. Power is just as distinct from the church of God as steam is distinct from the engine that it moves, or as life is distinct from the earth that seems to bring it forth.

The third class of people are those who realize this and have learned that "Power belongeth unto God," and that it is only as we have power from on high that we have spiritual power at all.

In the early days of the church's history, all the disciples belonged to the third class. The promise that the Spirit of God should be given to these disciples meant a definite thing to them. It meant nothing less than this: that the impossible should become possible, and that they should have power for whatever they were given to do. They knew what the Holy Ghost and power of the Holy Ghost meant. It meant "The power that had made psalmists and prophets and law-givers;" it meant the power that had caused Moses to break the chains that bound the enslaved people of God; it meant the power that had enabled Joshua to lead them in triumph into the promised land, and had stayed the sun and moon at his word of command until God had given the victory to Israel; it meant that which had been as a coal of fire from off God's altar to Isaiah; it meant that which made the sword of Gideon the sword of Almighty God; it meant that which made the word of Daniel mightier than the word of a king and a thousand of his lords. And they had need of some such power as this. The task that had been given them was a hard one—nay, it was an impossible one. As Arthur has said in his Tongue of Fire, it was a new religion and a poverty-stricken one, without a history, without a priesthood, without a college, without a patron. It had no presses; it had no literature; it had none of our modern means of influencing masses of men. It was cast solely on the one instrument of the tongue, and in that respect it was destitute of the wisdom of the Greek and of the skill of the scribe. It was seldom favored with an opportunity of addressing the same congregations or the same individuals. It was destitute of prestige; it was contemptible in numbers; it was rustic in manners and thwarted by circumstances. With only its two sacraments and its tongue of fire, on it went, and on, overturning its enemies and advancing the name of the Lord, from the day when, in the upper chamber, that little band heard the sound as of a mighty rushing wind, and down from heaven, through the roof, came tongues of fire that rested upon them. Their emblem was a tongue of fire—man's voice, God's truth; man's speech, God's inspiration; a human agent and the divine power. And this power was adequate for their impossible task. It was able to transform these disciples, who, before they received it, were as timid as sheep, until they were as brave as lions. "It had power to make the man who trembled at the

word of a maid-servant until he had de-
nied his Master, charge home upon the
rulers of the Jews, the murder of Jesus,
until they cried in deep concern.: 'Men
and Brethren, What shall we do?'"

I do not think I ever realized the mean-
ing of this emblem of fire until .I thought
of it in connection with the great fire
which I witnessed in the city of Boston.
I remember on that awful night, standing
on one of the busiest corners of the whole
city. A boy at school, I had come into
the city and had passed under the ropes
which held the crowd back from the fire,
and I stood near the place where the flames
were rapidly destroying one of those great
buildings. I remember how the fire came
to the corner of the street, and how it
seemed as if it had no power to go far-
ther. There it was, playing with the
building, while it burned out the wood-
work that was in it. But on the other
side of the street all was dark and dead.
There seemed to be no ray of light
and no spark of fire. Then suddenly,
almost without warning, this mighty force

overleaped the street and the building on
the other side burst into flames; and then,
just as when a match is touched to the
shavings that fill the stove, with a great
roar the fire swept through the block of
stone and brick and iron until it melted
at its touch. It seemed as though in a
few short moments the heart of that city
had vanished at the touch of this awful
element. This is the emblem that is given
to the church of God—the tongue of fire.

Was this power needed only for primary
conquest? Was it a special gift designed
for the founders and the founding of Christianity? Can God's work now be successfully prosecuted without it, and are
we now to depend on human wisdom, human learning, human experience and human energy? Has the day of miraculous
spiritual power passed by? Can any influence in this day of our great advance-
ment reach men—can it penetrate minds,
can it search hearts, can it burn dross,
can it melt prejudice, can it consume sin,
can it refine character—save the touch of
the fire that fell on Pentecost? Do we

not say, "No, there is no other influence," with our lips, while we say, "Yes" with our lives? Do we not pray as though we were dependent upon the Holy Ghost, and then live and plan and work as though we were dependent only on ourselves?

I am an optimist of the optimists. I believe there has never dawned upon the church of God a brighter day than this upon which we are here assembled; but I believe that when a church door swings open, when a prayer is offered or a song is sung or a sermon is preached, and these things are not inspired by the Spirit of God, they are useless. Nay, more, I believe that they are a curse. Churches multiply and ministers increase, but the shining face and the burning tongue are far to seek and hard to find. Some one has well said that on the day of the Pentecost one sermon converted three thousand souls, but that today it seems as though it took three thousand sermons to convert one soul. We have our cathedrals and temples and tabernacles and churches and chapels; we build our seminaries and colleges and schools and asylums and hospitals, all in the name of Jesus Christ. We have the wisdom of the ancients with the genius and the energy of the nineteenth century. No people ever sat better clothed, with better brains, and listened in their churches to words of more profound wisdom than we of today. We have our pray nights and our play nights, and a society for almost every purpose under heaven. We found our Young Men's Christian Associations; and then in a few short years it seems in many a place as if they had turned to the purpose of culturing men's bodies, rather than saving their souls. The great Christian Endeavor movement springs up in a night; and yet there are many spiritual souls that thank God for all that has been done and is being done by this great movement, that are tonight in deep spiritual travail that the work which God gives you to do as a society may be made and kept spiritual in all its aims and methods and developments. We have our vast missionary equipment, so that today six thousand missionaries of Jesus Christ have been telling the story of the cross; but still Ethiopia stretches out her hands in vain unto God, and the heathen in his blindness bows down to wood and stone. The church of God needs something, the church of God must have something more than she has today, with all her prestige and all her energy. She needs the upper chamber, she needs the tarrying at Jerusalem, she needs the power of the Holy Ghost, she needs a continued Pentecost; and nothing less than this can bring to her the slightest possible particle of power.

If Christianity today is independent of the Holy Ghost, let us state it plainly. Nay, let us state the contrary. "If there were a religion today that had the doctrines and all the ordinances of the New Testament and yet without the baptism of the Holy Ghost, it would not be Christianity;" it would be something else. What is needed is the power that came at Pentecost to speak to men in their own tongues, until you can touch the proud man and the sensual man, the

weak man and the avaricious man, as you
speak to him in the words of the tongue
that came at Pentecost.

There is no more fallacious saying than
that "Truth is mighty and must prevail."
Truth is not mighty. Men crucified the
One who justly said: "I am the Truth."
No word of our own poet was ever truer
than when he said that truth was—

> "—forever on the scaffold,
> Wrong forever on the throne,
> Yet that scaffold sways the future,
> And behind the dim unknown
> Standeth GOD within the shadow,
> Keeping watch above His own."

The power is not in the truth.   The
power is not in the Bible.   The power is
in God, as manifested to us by the Holy
Ghost.—"The sword of the Spirit" is *the
sword of the Spirit,* and without the Spirit's hand it is as useless as any other
handless sword. Nay, more, it will be
turned against the impious hand that
touches it save in the power and mission
of the Holy Ghost.

And yet God has not left Himself without witness.   "The eyes of the Lord run

to and fro throughout the whole earth to show Himself strong in behalf of them whose heart is perfect toward Him," and He has found such people. He found that man, Luther—Oh, how He looked through those dark centuries until He found him; and when He found him, He took this man and hurled him like a thunderbolt until He had brought to nothing the might and the wisdom of the impious blasphemers and hypocrites of that day. God looked for such a man in England until he found John Wesley, and gave him his half a million—nay, his tens of millions, of souls for his spiritual confidence in Jesus·Christ. God looked for such a man until he found Whitefield—a man destitute of much, but having a voice that was used as God's voice, and the tongue of fire touched and burned and melted men until, by the tens of thousands, they turned unto God. He looked for such a man until he found Finney. There was a time when Mr. Finney came into one of the factories at New York Mills, near Utica. As he came near the place where two girls were employed trying to mend a thread they began to laugh. As he came nearer, they began to cry and could not go on with their work, their hands trembled so. This man of .God came nearer to them and they sank down upon the seats before them, while the tears rained down their faces, so mightily were they convicted of their sin by the power of the Holy Ghost. Others were touched by the sight. The proprietor of the mill, who was present, though an unconverted man, said to the superintendent: "Stop the mill; it is more important that our souls shall be saved than this factory should run." The gate was immediately shut down, and the work stopped. A great and powerful meeting was held in the place at once and there that day, by the spiritual contact of the presence of that man of God, there were three or four hundred souls crying out: "God be merciful to us sinners."

When I was a pastor, one of my parishioners was the venerable Dr. Labaree, who was for many years president of Mid-

dlebury college. He told me that fifty
years ago, when he was a boy in Phillips
academy, at Andover, there was a young
man there who was so stupid that he could
not pass the examinations. He staid there
until some of his fellow-students had gone
out and taken the college course and come
back to the theological seminary across
the way. And yet that young man, so
stupid that he could not be admitted to
any college in the land, had more spiritual
power than all the rest of the students that
were in the academy with him. He had
no thought but of God, and he was filled
with Almighty God. After a while the
professors thought that, as he seemed so
consecrated, they would put a parenthesis
around the college and take him into the
theological seminary. They thought
that perhaps he would have a natural
taste for systematic theology, church history, Hebrew and all the rest of it; but,
poor fellow, it was all Hebrew to him.
And yet that man in the theological seminary was used to do more for God than
all the theological students and all the

professors and all the ministers and all
the church people in all the town of Andover. He went down to a little factory
village and started a Sunday School, and
there thirty or forty people turned to
God. He started another, and there a
score or more of people came to Christ.
He went over to Lawrence and founded a
Sunday School in that city that I believe
to-day has grown to be a flourishing and
powerful church. When the time came
for the students to leave Andover for their
summer vacation, there came a sum-
mons from a place in New Hampshire—
no; it was not from a place; it was from
one woman. She said. "I am the only
person in this town that believes in God.
We have no Bible; we have no Sabbath,
and we have no God. Can you not send
some one to us from your seminary who
will preach to us the word of life?" No
one of the students wanted to go, except
this man, and he thought it was just the
thing for which he had been waiting. The
professors did not know whether to license
him or not; but they finally concluded .

POWER FROM ON HIGH.

that he could not do a great deal of harm in six months, and so he was licensed for six months and sent into that town. He died soon after; but—and I give you this on the word of President Labaree—he did not die until he had won to Jesus Christ every man and woman and child in that township with the exception of one man, and he moved away soon after.

The question that concerns us in this connection is this: Are these exceptional cases, or are they given to us as examples? Here is what the greatest preacher said: "I am the least of the apostles; I am not meet to be called an apostle because I persecuted the church of God; but by the grace of God I am what I am, and that grace which was bestowed upon me was not in vain, for I labored more abundantly than they all; and yet not I, but the grace of God, which was with me." And this apostle says to us to-day: "God is able to make all grace abound toward you, that ye always, having all sufficiency in all things, may abound unto every good work."

The next question concerns the characteristics of spiritual power. What is it? It is nothing less than the life of God manifested through human character. There is no power that can create life except life; and this power finds its greatest exemplification in the life and words of Jesus Christ. He spoke those words two thousand years ago, and they have been sown and re-sown a million times, and yet they are vital for the production of life to-day. His power consisted in His consecration. It consisted in the fact that He came not to do His own will but the will of Him who sent Him, and so it pleased the Father to be glorified in the Son. This is the One who has said to us: "Greater works than I have done shall ye do," and "Whatsoever ye shall ask in My name that will I do." "Without Me ye can do nothing,"—not something, not little; "Ye can do *nothing*." Paul says: "I can do all things, through Christ, which strengtheneth me." "As the branch cannot bear fruit of itself except it abide in the vine, no more can ye except ye abide in Me." The Holy Spirit is not a freak of the Divine nature. He is the Divine nature itself manifested in power, in proportion as God is manifested in character and in life. Andrew Murray, one of the most spiritual writers of our time, has well said: "We want to get possession. of the power and use it. God wants the power to get possession of us and use us. If we give ourselves to the power to rule in us, the power will give itself to us to rule through us." The soldier joins the army not to get power but that the nation's power may be manifested in him and through him. There is no more distressing sign at this day than that so many people are ready to stand up in their places—consecrated people in a measure—and say: "I want to be used." It may be just as cursed an ambition to want to be used as to want to have money or to want to have one's pride fulfilled. What you and I need to have as an ambition is not to be used, but to be filled. The highest place is not that of the busy servant; it is that of the waiting

servant; it is that of the standing servant
Elijah used to call himself the standing
servant of God. "As the LORD God liveth," he would say, "before whom I stand."
In the Oriental countries to-day, princes
or men of wealth, will have at least one
servant who always stands erect in his
master's presence, in order that when he
speaks the servant need not even arise in
order to be ready to do his bidding"
Elijah meant that he never sat down
in God's presence, in order that when
God spoke he might run with the greater
celerity. If I were a merchant with such
a business that I had to employ several
errand boys, I should not regard that boy
as the most helpful or effective, who was
continually leaving his place and running
to me with the request that I should use
him. The thing that I would want from
those boys would be that they should be
ready to do what I told them to do—nothing more and nothing less. If they tried
to do more, or even wanted to do more,
they would be as harmful as though they
wanted or tried to do less.

"The strong man's strength to toil for Christ,
    The fervent preacher's skill,
I sometimes wish; but better far
    To be just what God will.
No service in itself is small,
    None great, through earth it fill;
But that is small that seeks its own,
    And great that seeks God's will."

You may remember the story of the blowing up of the rocks that were in the channel called Hell Gate, in the East River, that separates Long Island sound from the ocean. General Newton worked for years and years until at last he had the cavern made and stored with explosives, and the line, the magic wire, run from the explosives to the bank. Then, sitting upon the bank, he called to him his daughter Mary, a little child two years of age, and taking her upon his lap he told her to press that magic button. The little girl put forth her hand and pressed upon the button at her father's word, and instantly there came the mighty sound, the upheaval of the earth, and rocks and water, and the channel was partially free. Helplessness itself was that little - maiden, but power itself was the father on whose knee she rested. Oh, child of utter weakness, if thou wouldst but place thyself within the Father's love, the Father's thought, the Father's plan, then indeed would the Father's power flow through thy weakness until thou shouldst rend the rocks of pride and prejudice and passion; and even the gates of hell should not prevail against thee.

We come now to the very last question, and I beg of you to listen to it: How can we get spiritual power? WE CANNOT GET IT. No man ever possessed it; no man ever owned it; no man ever used it. It is a question, not of our getting power, but of God getting us; not of our using God, but of God using us. The disciples were not told to pray for power nor to seek for power. They were told to wait for the Holy Ghost. We know that they waited for ten days and then the Holy Ghost came. What did they do in those ten days? What does "waiting" mean? I wish you could have seen us as we waited at Gardner, Massachusetts, for our train—the excursion train, that was half an hour late. We stood upon the track, a score or more, and looked down the iron rail to see if the train was not coming. If you had asked some of us to go across the street to get a hundred dollars, I do not believe that we would have done it. We would not move; we must stay there; we were doing just one thing, and it is the one thing with which we cannot do anything else—we were wait-ing. The most intense occupation in the universe is to wait. To wait for the Holy Ghost is, not to do nothing, but it is to *wait*,—not having the possibility of anything else touching the mind with any allurement; it is to wait for God. Some one has said that the disciples had to wait ten days, and that there were ten days in which they were being filled with the Holy Ghost. That is a mistake. They were not waiting ten days to be filled; they were waiting to be emptied. Dr. Gordon has reminded us that the wind always blows toward a vacuum. If you could exhaust the air from this great tabernacle to-night, and then could make a crevice in it, you would hear the wind come whistling in. And so, in that upper chamber, the disciples were being emptied and a vacuum was being made. The son of thunder was emptied of the thunder, that he might be filled with love. The doubting Thomas was emptied of his doubt that he might be filled with light. The presumptuous and vacillating Peter was emptied of his presumption and his fickleness that he might be filled with all the power of God. And then there came the sound as of a mighty rushing wind, and God came upon them and used them.

A great mesmerist told me one day that the one qualification under which he could mesmerize people was that they should have vacant minds. If a man might pour his mind into the vacant mind of another creature until he should think his thought and do his will, what might not God do if only He could have vacant spirits into which He could pour Himself. The great condition of power is to be emptied of self and to be filled

with God; to renounce self and to appro-
priate God; to be dead unto self but to
be alive unto God by the power of the
Holy Ghost. "God has chosen the foolish
things of this world to confound the
things that are wise, and God has chosen
the weak things of this world to confound the things that are mighty, and the
base things of this world and things that
are despised hath God chosen, yea, and
things that are not, to bring to naught
things that are." "Things that are *not*,"
hath God chosen. That was why He
chose Jesus Christ, who "made himself of
no reputation," and became obedient unto death, as he humbled himself; there-
fore, hath God highly exalted Him, and
that is the only way that God will ever
exalt any one of us. It was only when
Luther could say: "Martin Luther does
not live here: Jesus Christ lives here,"
that God could use Luther. And it was
only as Paul could say: "I am crucified
with Christ, nevertheless I live, and yet
no longer I, but Christ liveth in me"
that Paul could be used of God. It is

only as you and I can say the same that he
can use us, even in the faintest degree.

I used to pray for power. I thank God
that I never pray for power now. I used to
pray for power alone, and then, I prayed
for power with humility, and then, for
power through humility; but I thank
God that I came to learn at last this
one thing, that the only prayer that touches power will be the prayer that says:
"Thy will be done in me, even as it is
done in heaven."   The place of privilege
where we can say: "God is mine," is
only where we can say: "I am His;"
and we cannot truly say: "Whom I serve,"
until we have said: "Whose I am."   Let
God take us; let us be willing to do the
will of God, and He will lead us to a
mighty faith.   And when you shall come
to that place where you seek not your
own, but where your heart is set on God
and where the eyes of God as they run to
and fro throughout all the earth shall see
you, then there shall come to you the
mighty power of an appropriating faith
until you shall reach up and take hold on all

the fullness of God. You will be God's; God will be yours; all that there is of God will be poured into you—nothing held back—nothing of wisdom, nothing of love, nothing of tenderness, nothing of power — all will be yours— all things, whether Paul or Apollos or Peter or the world or life or death or things present or things to come, all will be yours; and you may go forth without one particle of hesitation to do as the one of old did in the power of the Holy Ghost, "to be set over kingdoms, to root out, to pull down, to destroy, to overthrow, and to build and to plant."

Some of you have seen the great picture that was painted by Muncakszy of the Christ. That picture was being exhibited in Canada, at Toronto, I think, and there came a rude, rough, wicked sailor to see it. He entered the room at the time of day when there were no others there; and paying his money to the woman who sat inside the door, he came in and stood for a moment, looking at the canvas as though he would glance at it and go away. But as he looked, he could not turn. He stood there with his eyes fixed on that central figure of majesty and love. In a few moments, he took off his hat and let it fall upon the floor. After a few moments more he sat down upon a seat, and then he reached down and picked up a book that described the picture, and began to read; and every few seconds his eyes would turn toward the canvas and toward the figure of Christ. The lady who sat by the door saw him lift up his hand and wipe away some tears. Still he sat; five, ten, fifteen, sixty minutes went by, and still the man sat there as though he could not stir. At last he rose, and coming softly and reverently toward the door, he hesitated, to take one last look, and said to the woman who sat there: "Madam; I am a rough, wicked sailor; I have never believed in Christ; I have never used His name except in an oath; but I have a Christian mother, and my old mother begged me today before I went to sea, to go and look at the picture of the Christ. To oblige her I said I would come and I have come. I did not believe that anybody believed in Christ; but as I have looked at that form and that face I have thought that some man must have believed in Him, and it has touched me, and I have come to believe in Him, too. I am going out from this time to be a believer in Jesus Christ and a follower of His." Oh, beloved, as I heard that story, the tears came unbidden to my eyes, and my heart glowed with a mighty longing. I thought if a poor, weak man, living himself in a godless land, could take his brush and preach on canvas, and cause our Christ to glow upon it, until a rough, rude, wicked, licentious man should be won to believe in Him, what might not my God do if he might paint Christ in me—nay, if he might reproduce Christ in a human life, that the life might be Christ's and that men might come to believe on Him.

Dr. Field has given us a picture which has been oft repeated, of the lighting of the torches in the holy sepulchre at Easter time. The building is crowded; I suppose, by a thousand or more of the members of the Greek church. The patriarch comes. All is darkness; but they make way in the throng as he passes through. He goes through the curtain, into the place where the body of Jesus is supposed to have lain, and waits. Not a word, not a sound, scarcely a breath; a full hour passes by, and the breathless throng wait there in the great darkness. Suddenly there is a movement. Suddenly they see a spark, and out comes the patriarch from the sepulchre, out from the darkness, bringing with him light, a torch that is lighted. Instantly there are a hundred hands stretched out for it, and they take the torch and pass it from hand to hand; torches are stretched out until they reach it and are kindled from it, until a thousand torches burn with the light that comes from the tomb of Christ. Out into the streets of Jerusalem, out into the highways and byways they go, and other torches are lighted from theirs until the whole land glows with the fire that comes from the tomb of the Savior. In these closing moments let me ask you to come with me into the place of the death of Jesus Christ. May God kill the ambition in us, the selfishness, the pride, the world in us, until we shall be crucified with Christ. May the very One that laid in that sepulchre light our torches to-night and hold His torch out to this great throng until the light of God and the tongue of fire shall touch you, and you, and you, and you, that we may go out into the streets of this city and into this great state and along these rivers and the iron highways, to the north, the south, the east, the west, to Maine, to California; to Texas, to Canada—nay, until we go across the sea to India, to Africa, to the isles of the sea, and the whole world shall be touched with the light of God and the fire of Pentecost from the grave of our Lord Jesus Christ. The death of self and the life of God I pray may come unto us now, and as we go, let us go with bowed heads, saying reverently: "Not unto us, not unto us, but unto Thy name give glory," "it is not by might, not by power, but by Thy Spir-

it," oh, Thou Lord of Hosts, and as we
go, let us go with uplifted hearts, sing-
ing our doxology, "Thine is the kingdom,
and the power and the glory, forever and
ever.   Amen."

WS - #0033 - 100524 - C0 - 229/152/2 - PB - 9781331734321 - Gloss Lamination